W9-CBR-285

BRIEFCASE TO DIAPER ★ BAG

A Mother's Journey
To Find Balance At Home

Katie Kelley Dorn

Nantucket Publications
Minnetonka, MN

Library of Congress Cataloging in Publication Data

Dorn, Katie Kelley. 1960-
   Briefcase to diaper bag : a mother's journey to find balance at home /
Katie Kelley Dorn.
    p.   cm.
    ISBN 0-9640435-1-3 : $10.95
    1. Working mothers. 2. Married women–Employment. I. Title.
HQ759.48.D65   1995
306.874'3–dc20   94-9990   CIP

Cover design and illustrations are original artwork produced by Jodi Anderson,
Minneapolis, MN.

Layout by Wendy Wright, *wrighters, ink.,* St. Paul, MN.

Printed in the United States of America.

To Dave, Kelley, Charlie and Janie
for bringing joy to my journey.

★ Table of Contents ☞

PROLOGUE

I have often heard that parents are their children's greatest teachers. I tend to think it's the other way around.

Tinkering with my computer one afternoon, my oldest daughter started working on a "book," like Mommy. She diligently plunked away at the keyboard - typing, deleting, refining - until she was ready to print. Hot off the press, she whisked her paper off for some crayoned illustrations of colored hearts, flowers, and rainbows. Proudly she presented her masterpiece to me with a smile. "Read it," she demanded.

Roses are red, Vilotes are blu. If you want sumthin bad enuf.
It will com tru.

"That's wonderful, honey. Did you write that yourself?"

"No. I heard it on Lamb Chop."

"What do you think it means?" I asked.

She looked at me hesitantly, "I think it means if you try hard enough, you can do it. Like when I stopped sucking my thumb or learned to ride my bike without training wheels. I wanted to do it so bad, I kept trying till I did it. What do you think it means?"

"Exactly that." I smiled.

Who needs Zig Ziglar, Tommy Thompson or Anthony Robbins when you've got kids around? With incredible honesty and insight, our children constantly amaze me by whittling down life's complicated philosophies into simple lessons.

Two years ago I traded in my briefcase for a diaper bag to stay home with our preschool age children. After ten years in the corporate world, I was anxious about redefining myself from working mom to at-home mom. I was scared. Would I lose myself at home with kids all day?

Yes, for awhile. But by quieting myself and listening to the insights of my children, I've started to whittle down my fears and insecurities into a simple lesson.

If you want sumting bad enuf it will com tru.

It is starting to come true for me. More than anything I want to be the best mother I can be for our children, without risking my marriage or losing myself. And after two years at home, I've begun to figure out how to find balance at home with my three young children.

As a result, I'm not so anxious and impatient anymore. I've always been in love with my kids, but now I've fallen in love with full-time motherhood. Here's my story.

★ x ☾

CHAPTER ONE

Starting a Lifelong Journey

The room broke into thunderous applause. I, along with 25 other college women, had a new heroine of the week. Our speaker for the "Women in Leadership Summer Internship Program" in Chicago was another successful businesswoman sharing her story of how she made it in the business world: MBA, networking, landing a job in product management at a top consumer food corporation, working hard and working smart to rise up to VP level in just five years. In my eyes she was a goddess.

It was thrilling to think that could be me in just a few years. I was eager. I was young and optimistic. And I could hardly wait to grab my briefcase and hop onto the fast track so it could all happen to me.

Never in my wildest dreams did I think that ten years later I would be hopping right off the fast track to stay home to raise my children. Women of our generation could have it all, kids and career. We had options that repressed housewives of the fifties and sixties hadn't had. They had been forced into the bondage of home and children. Lucky for us, they had broken out from the home and forged ahead into the corporate world demanding equal jobs and equal pay. They had fought the battles and laid the groundwork for us, the next decade of women, to rise to the top. If I traded in my career aspirations to go back to the home front, their trailblazing would have been fruitless.

I felt fortunate to be graduating from college in the early 1980s, because I knew that for me it wouldn't be a matter of *either/or.* This was the decade of the SuperMom. I could have it all.

Seven years later, on June 22, 1988, my husband and I had our first daughter, Kelley Elizabeth Dorn. This tiny little creature was perfect. We examined every inch of her skin, every crevice between her toes, the tiny fingernails on her hands. I kept pulling up her shirt and looking at her new, scabby belly button. That cord had been our connection, her lifeline, for nine months. It was a miracle. She was a miracle. She may have begun from our seeds, but her creation was a work of divine wonder that really had very little to do with us.

I remember staring at her for hours. I couldn't believe she was ours. I was her mother. We were her parents. She was coming home with us. She had a whole life of "first times" ahead of her that were long ago memories for me. Her first smile...her first steps...her first words...her first bike ride...her first day of school... her first date...her first day of college. I panicked with the thought that these first times would all too soon be memories for her, too.

This was a first time for me. I had never before felt motherly instincts pulsing through my blood. I pulled her close and stared into her eyes. Yes, I felt innately protective. But the deep bond and love I expected to feel for her wasn't instant. It was more powerful than that. I would find in the coming days that it grew slowly and deeply. It swelled with each nighttime feeding, together in the dark and the quiet, her warm breath upon me before she clasped on to nurse, her soft cheek up close to my skin and her wide eyes staring into mine as she clung to me. As the days and weeks passed, I was overwhelmed by the power of my attachment and love for her. In the shadow of the night as we rocked back and forth, I felt like I had been reborn right along with her. My career seemed miles away. I wasn't sure how my tidy little professional life would fit into my new walk with motherhood.

Thus began my journey to redefine myself. I was a mother. I was a spouse. I was a career person with goals and dreams. How did those all mesh together? I wished I had thought to ask my career goddess these questions back in the summer of 1980!

Before I had even begun to ponder these questions, let alone sleep through the night, it was twelve weeks later. It was time for me to return to work full time. I didn't even allow myself to think about the option of staying home with Kelley. My sister and I had just sold our marketing company to a large corporation and had signed a multi-year employment agreement which we had to fulfill. So it was back to the rat race.

For almost three years, and through the birth of our second child, Charles Ernest Dorn, I tried to balance a full-time career and motherhood. As I ran between home and work, I unraveled the myth of the SuperMom. For me, SuperMom became a synonym for super-stressed, super-guilty and super-tired.

I was tired of the 60-hour work weeks, the out-of-town business trips, the dinner meetings. Tired of less than accommodating attitudes of corporations toward families and part-time management work. Tired of feeling like whenever I was at work, I should be home with my kids, and whenever I was at home, I should be at work. I was trapped in a world of mediocrity, doing everything halfway. I'm the type of person who likes to do everything to its best, and I couldn't. I felt split right down the middle.

Two years ago, in the hope of becoming whole again, I hopped off the fast track. I traded in my briefcase for a diaper bag so I could dedicate myself to the task of raising our two preschool age children, with a third on the way.

So, how does a career-minded, goal-driven working parent adjust to at-home parenthood? The hundreds I've asked have said the same things over and over again. It's hard. Someone should write a book about it.

I'm one of those parents, and I decided to write a book about it.

Every few months I touch base with a friend of mine who moved to Texas. She's an attorney with two young children, and she is contemplating the briefcase trade-in herself. Every time we talk she asks, "So, how is it? Do you like being at home full time with the kids? Do you think I should do it?"

And each time I answer, "The kids are great, most of the time. I love it. But, if you really want to know, today's not the greatest day to ask. I'm keeping very busy, but I guess I'm still adjusting."

After two years at home I'm *still* giving the same answer. I'm adjusting.

How I'm adjusting is what I want to share in this book . And knowing how little time parents have for extra reading, I've attempted to tell my story so it can be read during the average child's nap time—if you're lucky enough to have a child who naps.

WHAT THIS BOOK IS AND ISN'T

I realize that I'm fortunate to have the choice to stay home when many parents do not. And many parents who do have a choice decide to keep pursuing a full-time career outside the home because that is the right choice for them and for their family. So this book is definitely not a preachy sermon outlining the virtues of becoming a stay-at-home parent. My motto is that a happy parent is a good parent, and striking that balance between work, family, and self is the key to happiness for every parent, whether working outside or in the home.

This book is also not a how-to book for every parent who decides to stay home with kids. I don't have any formula to make the transition a breeze. I just wanted to share my story for three reasons:

1. I NEEDED A CATHARSIS

Part of my dilemma in staying home full time was that I didn't have a good creative outlet. I wanted to be home with my kids without losing touch with my personal goals and aspirations. I didn't want to trap myself in the bondage from which house-wives of the '50s and '60s felt they had to escape. I wanted more for myself at home.

Sure, I've mastered the art of making cute Play Dough animals, and I can make a doozy of a puppet from a brown paper sand-wich bag. But I needed a challenge that would validate my sense of self outside my kids.

However, where could I find a challenging career where I could work part time and make enough money to pay for child care for three preschoolers? And it could not be a job that would conflict with Kelley's preschool schedule or carpooling to gymnastics. And I definitely wanted two weeks off at Christmas as well as the entire summer.

I found my answer when I decided to write and publish this book from home. It was a challenging career alternative that actually fit within my job criteria.

2.   I NEEDED A FOCUS AT HOME

I'm writing this book for me. I still struggle with my transition from briefcase to diaper bag. The first snow fell last week in Minneapolis, and I went into a deep funk. The thought of an entire winter holed up with my three kids under the age five scared me.

Sure, I have those days that are close to perfect, days where all three kids actually act like they like each other and like me on the same day. Those are the glorious days that make it all worthwhile. But more times than not at least one of us is crabby, or tired, or whiny, and I need an attitude adjustment to stay focused on being a positive and happy mom at home with my kids. Because if I can't find balance and contentment at home, I'll fire myself as their full-time caretaker and get a job again outside the home.

So, by writing a book I forced myself to think through my life at home and formulate an outline of how I can stay positive and happy doing what I chose to do — build a career as an at-home mother.

3. A HUMOROUS LOOK AT LIFE FOR OTHER PARENTS

My hope is that through this book other parents can relate and laugh along with me. Since I've been home with our kids, there have been days when I've so longed for adult conversation that I've actually sprinted to the mailbox to chit-chat with our mail-carrier. As tragic as that may sound, I have often wondered if I was the only at-home parent with these waves of loneliness and unsettled feelings?

But then I'd have a moment of enlightenment, like when I was talking to my friend who confessed that for her, too, seeing one hand-addressed letter amidst the bills and junk mail can be the highlight of her day. I chimed right in, "That describes me to a tee! I was ecstatic last week when I got an invitation to a Tupperware party. The scary thing is that I went and loved it!" As we laughed and shared that moment, I realized I wasn't alone.

Hopefully, by reading my story you can have moments like those, too. And you can take parts of my story, meld them with your own life, and continue your journey to find balance in your walk with parenthood, knowing you're not alone.

CHAPTER TWO

My Day of Reckoning

WASHING AN ELEPHANT

Two years ago, after almost ten years as a career woman, I dove into full-time motherhood like I do most things. Quickly.

My mother says I've always been like that. She says that if I decided to wake up one day and wash an elephant, I'd get out the hose and just start squirting.

When I was in high school she always used to ask me, "Why don't you take your time, Kate? Go slowly. Think things through and plan a little bit before you dive in."

"I guess I just like to learn by doing," I'd boast. "I might make a mistake once, but I'll get it right the next time."

For my first months of being home with our kids, I didn't get it right the next time. I made the same mistakes over and over again. I was so overwhelmed by the major changes I had taken on at home that I couldn't even take time to question whether or not I was heading in the right direction.

With a snap of a finger my life had taken a 180 degree turn. Some of the changes were visible. I went from nylons to sweat pants, from computer programs to Barney, from P&L statements to finger-paints. At the end of my first week at home, I was craving a lunch out with my friends from the office. I could almost taste a chicken sandwich with fries from the Loon Cafe. I was horrified to realize my lunches all week had consisted of peanut butter and honey sandwich crusts. I had even stooped to the dreaded low-point I swore I would never reach; picking off and actually eating leftover macaroni and cheese from the baby's highchair tray.

But those transformations were obvious and expected. The changes that really surprised me were the physical and emotional demands of raising two young children day in and day out while I was pregnant with our third. After a day at home I was dizzy from the up and down the stairs four times an hour; the zipping up and zipping down of jackets; the changing in and out of clothes; the constant bending to tie a shoe, wipe a nose, or pick up a toy; the in and out of different car-seats four times for each child on each outing in each day; the back-and-forth to the refrigerator for more of this and more of that during every meal. It seemed endless.

I had imagined that staying home with kids would be an escape from the petty employee complaints and bickering that drove me crazy at work. But all day long I was on an emotional roller coaster. I dealt with whining, tantrums, tattle-taling, and semi-schizophrenic behavior. We'd be enjoying a happy moment around the lunch table when out of the blue Charlie would have a complete melt-down before my eyes for no apparent reason. It would take me five minutes to figure out it was because I gave him the blue cup instead of the yellow cup. Even after I gave him the yellow cup, there was no consoling him. It was enough to drive me crazy.

At the end of each day I would collapse into a chair in our den, and thank God that I had simply survived. Whether I had done a good job or not wasn't even an issue.

I quickly realized that I had made the hardest career move I'd ever maneuvered in my life, yet probably the most important. I felt ill-prepared for the challenges I faced in raising well-adjusted, happy kids. One minute I was the happy homemaker, and the next I was totally losing control. After one month at home, it seemed that going back to work outside the home would be a welcome relief, for me and the kids.

I had become so indentured to the physical and emotional demands of my kids, I began to lose myself. I was sucked into full-time motherhood so quickly, I never had a chance to figure out how I really wanted to do it and who I wanted to be.

SETTING THE STAGE

For months I had been trying to wash an elephant without thinking it through, until my day of reckoning.

Let me set the stage for this day, the day I came to terms with the fact that my life as full-time, at-home mother was lacking something, and that something was me. The day I realized my transition from briefcase to diaper bag had left some major voids in my life. Voids that I needed to fill.

Picture this, if you will...

I was thirty weeks pregnant with our third child. I was not even close to feeling that "glow" of pregnancy you read about. I felt fat, much bigger than I remembered being when I was pregnant with our first two. I had wretched heartburn and couldn't eat anything but frozen yogurt or crackers without feeling like I was having cardiac arrest. Usually I opted for the frozen yogurt, complete with Butterfinger topping.

Needless to say, I kept getting bigger and bigger. My feet had swelled to a size 9 1/2 EEE. When I'd take off the only pair of shoes I could squeeze into (size 10 canvas slippers), I'd have huge red indentations all the way around my feet. Before children, I had worn a 7 narrow, the perfect foot by most standards. Those days were gone for good.

My sister Ginny offered a comforting thought. She reminded me that during my first two pregnancies, I had been busy working outside the home. This time around I was home with two kids, probably eating more and not getting as much exercise. That cheered me up a lot.

I was also coping with every woman's nightmare. I was growing my hair out. I had gotten a trendy short "do" after our second child was born. Charlie had been even more colicky than Kelley, our first, and there were many nights when neither my husband nor I slept more than a combined total of three hours. I had felt peaked and tired and needed a diversion. What better than a new haircut to perk me up? One month later I started the process of growing it back. Need I say more?

Outgrowing maternity clothes at 30 weeks was depressing enough, but add a year of bad hair days and barrettes on top of that, and it doesn't do much for your self-image.

On this particular day I had to go over to my sister Betsy's house to borrow some maternity clothes for a "girls'" weekend in Colorado. Dave had given me a frequent flier ticket for my birthday, and I was using it to visit some close college friends–my last getaway before the baby came.

Betsy had been home from the hospital with her third child for just two weeks. She was up nursing the baby every two hours, so I fully expected to just run in and out since she would undoubtedly be in a zombie-like state.

She answered the door looking fresh as a daisy, already back in her size 4 jeans.

"You look great." I tried my best to sound enthusiastic. I looked her over and said flatly, "I'd better try on those maternity tops. With all the frozen yogurt I've been consuming these days, I'm not so sure they'll fit."

I was begging for just one ego-boosting response. All she had to do was throw me a bone. That was our sisterly game. It was her turn to respond with, "Don't be silly. You look svelte. A wisp, a weed...like a pregnant Audrey Hepburn."

It wasn't there. My sister Betsy is as sweet as they come, but she couldn't lie. "Kate, you might perk up for this weekend if you primp a little bit. You need to feel better about yourself."

"I'm not a primper." I didn't attempt to sound enthusiastic.

"Do you think I just wake up looking like this?" she joked. " If you just fussed with your hair a little, you could actually have a hair-do of sorts. Come on upstairs. Let me take out those tragic barrettes and try the curling iron on those bangs. The kids can play in the basement."

She marched me upstairs, sat me down, and went to work. I was feeling better already. I never had been much of a primper, so maybe this was the pick-me-up I needed. I tried on a few of her cute maternity tops, and by the time I left that afternoon, I was feeling rather perky.

My plane to Colorado left at five that Friday afternoon. Dave came home early to take the helm for the weekend while I was off for my girls' weekend.

I wanted to make sure I got to the airport early. It was only November 9th and, thanks to the Halloween blizzard, there were 28 inches of snow on the ground. Even for Minnesota that's deep and that's early. The roads were all rutted with ice and driving was bad. I got to the airport with only a half hour to spare, parked in the underground garage, and ran to my gate. By the time I got there, I was sweating profusely. I had on my black snow tights, Dave's Sorrel snow boots (mine didn't fit), a big parka barely zipped over my bulging belly, hat, mittens — and my orange duffel bag swung over my shoulder.

I looked up and the "rather perky" was zapped right out of me. The gate area was packed with typical late Friday afternoon business commuters. The women seemed like a blur of Ann Taylor business suits, Liz Claiborne dresses, Hanes hosiery, low pumps, and sporty briefcases that weren't too businesslike. Through the blur emerged a cute pregnant mother. She wore a tailored maternity pantsuit and vogue flats. To top it off she had a darling short haircut. Her two perfectly dressed children sat by her side coloring as she hung up the phone from what was undoubtedly an important business call.

It was hard to believe that had been me just five months before. I used to travel on business, use a calling card, and carry a sporty briefcase. I had been a Preferred WorldPerks member on Northwest Airlines, for God's sake. I had pumps in five colors and my choice of flats. I had carried on stimulating conversations with the best of them.

It was at that precise moment I was sidetracked by the distinct smell of poop. I took a step back from the vogue pregnant mom and her two perfectly coifed children. Surely beneath their matching Gap Kids outfits was a mother-lode of diapers to be changed, and the stench was mighty strong. As I brushed my newly curled bangs off my forehead, the smell became overwhelming once again. That was when horror stuck. It was me. My hands reeked of poop. I had been in such a rush to get to the airport after changing Charlie's diaper, I had forgotten to wash my hands. The thought of it made me physically ill. Yet in a funny way it was as if the odor gave me the jolt I needed. The jolt to look at myself more clearly.

ASKING MYSELF THE QUESTION - COULD I REALLY HANDLE THIS?

I stood there, mortified, and started to take a good, long look at myself. And for the first time in months, I honestly and truly wanted to go back to my old life and career. I'd just do one of those "Bewitched" nose twitches, pitch my orange duffel bag for a sporty briefcase, and trade places with that vogue mom in the maternity pantsuit.

It had only been five months since my briefcase trade-in, and at that moment, I wasn't sure I liked what I had become. I felt empty, like I had lost sight of who I was and why I wanted to carry a diaper bag in the first place. I was becoming self-consumed with things of little import, like maternity clothes and curling irons. I was reacting to the demands of at-home motherhood without direction .

For five months I had been letting the days seize me instead of seizing each day. And in doing so, I was losing touch with my purpose and my vision of what I wanted to be as an at-home mother.

This was my day of reckoning. Was I really cut out for this, or could I have made the biggest mistake of my life?

CHAPTER THREE

Did I Trade In the Wrong Bag?

As I washed my hands off in the airport bathroom, I thought back just five months to when I had left work to be a full-time, at-home mom. I tried to remember, did I have it all? Should I trade my diaper bag back for my briefcase?

MY LIFE IN THE WORKING WORLD

Just five months earlier I had a challenging job managing 60 co-workers at the marketing company my sister Ginny and I had started, developed, and sold to a NYSE company.

I had a loving husband who did more around the house than most dads I knew. He had a fulfilling job in product management at a telecommunications company. And after

almost eight years of marriage, we still laughed a lot and truly loved being together.

We had two lights in our lives, our kids. Kelley, our daughter and first-born, was two-and-a-half going on twenty. Charlie, our son, was eight months old and just getting over the worst colic in history. It was amazing how cute we thought he was even when he cried seven hours a day. And I was just pregnant with our third child.

We had the superb nanny. Laurie came to our house every weekday from 7:30 am till 6:00 pm and brought her daughter Lexie, who became Kelley's soulmate and playmate.

Every day when I arrived home from work, the house looked better and cleaner than when I had left. The laundry was clean and folded like I imagined only Hazel folded laundry. All we had to do was take the neat little piles from our bed and put them away in our dresser.

I had a cleaning lady every week. I had a health club membership and worked out over lunch two or three times a week. We officed in the swanky warehouse district of downtown Minneapolis, and my commute in the carpool lane with my co-worker/neighbor was no more than 30 minutes, 20 minutes on a good day.

So did I have it all? Yes, if you want to include 100% eternal guilt. I couldn't fight it. It was an inherent part of my Catholic upbringing, and guilt punctuated each and every one of my waking hours.

Guilt for not spending enough time with the kids.
Monday through Friday I dressed them in the morning before rushing off to work. When I returned home sometime after 6:00 pm, Dave and I gave them a quick dinner, popped them in the bathtub, read them a couple of stories, and then put them to bed. On weekends between shopping, bill paying, chores, and church, we managed to squeeze in a little time for just hanging out with the kids.

Guilt for not having enough time for my husband or friends.
What had been squeezed out of my life entirely was time for Dave, time for our social life, and time for myself. Going out in the evening and leaving a baby-sitter with the kids, knowing they were spending over 60 hours a week with a nanny, made me feel guilty. Getting together on the weekend with a friend for a walk or lunch made me feel guilty. Recreational sports were games of the past. They took up too much time away from the kids.

Guilt for being mad at Dave for not having guilt feelings.
Did he give up golf, fishing, and outings with friends? No. And I was jealous of him. I wished I could take time for me. I knew I should take time for me. But I lived in guilt and neurotically counted the waking hours the kids spent with me each week versus the time they spent with the nanny. (Only waking hours counted. Sleeping hours were forced out of the equation in the

hope it would balance in my favor.)

Dave, like many '90s dads, compared himself with his father and thought, "Hey, my Dad was a great Dad, and I'm even more involved and more active in my kids' lives than my dad was in mine. I do more with them and spend more time with them." He then felt good about himself as a parent and wasn't guilt-ridden when he did take time for himself. (Plus, for some reason, Catholic guilt and martyrdom is not passed on generation to generation in the male sector as it is for females.)

For me, on the other hand, it was different, like it is for so many '90s moms who work full time outside the home. My standard was my mom, and when I compared myself with her I thought, "Hey, my mom was there for me. She was there making cookies for me when I got home from school. She was in my classroom, at my school events, and always at home to listen to my every crisis and question. So I guess I'm not doing as good a job with my kids as my mother did with me." Therefore, after a long week at work, I was paralyzed with guilt whenever I took even one iota of extra time away from the kids.

And it wasn't just guilt I was dealing with. As long as I can remember, I had always dreamt of having a family and raising a passel of children. And now that I was finally there, with two little ones, soon to be three, I felt like I was missing it all.

I missed the kids. I missed reading to them before they went down for naps and cuddling them when they got up. I would call home several times a day to chat with Laurie to see what they were up to, to hear what I was missing. I wanted to be with them and spend more time together. The years were flying by, and I knew I couldn't cram a week's worth of bonding into two weekend days. A lot went on during the 60 hours a week when Dave and I were at work. Sure, we tried having quality time, but the hours we spent at home were not necessarily our kids' "quality" hours. There was something to be said for a little more quantity of time.

During those 60 hours we were at work, we had the burden of arranging quality "child care" for our kids. We were lucky. We had a great nanny who came to our house, but for how long? She was our second nanny in a little over two years, and I was paranoid about losing her. I was certain she was planning to have another baby soon and worried that she'd leave us after that. Then we'd have to start the exhausting round of interviewing for another one, and good ones were so hard to find. What if, after all the interviewing, we ended up with a psycho, or a child-beater, or someone who was totally irresponsible? What about my guilt when either or both of the kids got sick? Even with our unusually good situation, the whole subject of child care was a huge, ongoing stress.

AGONIZING DECISIONS, PAINSTAKING CHOICES

So what was the answer to all this guilt and stress? To stay home full time? That scared me to death. What would I do all day? Who would I talk to? Would I lose my drive and my energy? I wanted to be home with the kids, yet I envisioned myself going crazy without the challenge and stimulation of work. Would I be a good and patient mother day in and day out, or would I rag at the kids all day until they just waited by the door for Dad to come home? I didn't have confidence that I was prepared for the full-time role of mother.

And I was scared as well about losing financial independence. The bottom line was that my salary helped make life comfortable for us. So even though we could manage financially on Dave's income, it would mean cutbacks. Goodbye to all the "perks" and extras.

I had also invested 10 years in my career and still had professional goals I wanted to reach. If I stayed home full time, would I have to forfeit my career aspirations? Or would there be a way for me to balance them from home?

And, aside from the career and financial aspects, what kind of example would I be to our kids if I stayed at home? Statistics about our generation show that both parents work harder for less disposable income, and that will intensify in the future. The reality is that our children will most likely have to work if and when they have children twenty years from now. I wanted to be a positive and realistic role model for our kids, and I wasn't sure I could do that staying home full time.

It's a generational thing. Part of the problem for parents of our generation is the contrast between how we were brought up and how we're bringing up our children. And our kids will be making the same kinds of contrasts. I just wasn't sure I wanted to pass on my guilt and neuroses to our children.

So after much thought and deliberation, Dave and I came up with a solution. It was ideal. I would go to the office just three days a week, and I would have office hours at home on Tuesday and Friday mornings from 8 to10, all at 75% of my current salary. We would keep our nanny four days a week so I could have the flexibility to meet a friend for lunch, have a "one-on-one" outing with one of the kids, or get my errands done early to free up more "quality" time on weekends. On the fifth "nanny-less" day, we could have family outings, especially if Dave could negotiate a four-day work week. Coupled with our three weeks of vacation, we would have lots more time with the kids, and yet still have the financial security and stimulation of work. It was a long shot, but worth a try.

I was actually pretty close to negotiating that exact scenario with the corporation that had acquired our company. So close that I was planning to talk to our nanny about it when, *BOOM!* The lid got blown off. The parent company decided it could run things on its own, without us! With the stroke of a pen we were history.

So the decision was staring me in the face. I had no more employee contract to fulfill. I was free to do what I had dreamt about doing for months, stay at home with the kids. But the reality of it all scared me. With the career, financial, and personal implications it would have on me and our family, I was terrified of making the leap. I put off making a final decision and stalled by looking for the ideal, part-time, challenging career.

A couple of weeks later Ginny and I were completing the paperwork to finalize our exit package from the company. One of the forms had a line on which I had to fill in "Occupation." I remember staring at the line. And staring. And staring.

And finally I took my pen in hand and filled in "Homemaker."

For me that was my moment of truth. I was going to make the big switch. I made a definitive choice and decided to give it a go. I traded in my briefcase for a diaper bag.

CHAPTER FOUR

I Never Thought I'd Miss Wearing Pumps

Re-Assessing my decision

Five months later, standing in the airport that Friday afternoon on my way to a college reunion — fat, pregnant and sweaty — I examined myself and my insecurities.

I reminded myself that I had made the choice that was right for me. I had given up the 60-hour work weeks, the travel schedules, the dinner meetings. I had opted for full-time momhood.

Yes, I envied the pregnant mom in the vogue pantsuit because she seemed able to do it all, career, kids, the whole shot. And she seemed happy. I couldn't do it all. I had

already discovered that.

If I had been successful in negotiating my "ideal" job, maybe a part-time career would have worked out. But on the other hand, I really wanted to be home when Kelley got home from preschool, when all the events of the morning were fresh in her mind. I wanted to carpool like the other moms. I wanted to be the one to hug our kids when they got up from their naps. I wanted to volunteer at school like my mom had. And I definitely wanted to experience full time with my kids for the whole Christmas season as well as the whole summer.

Some friends of mine do have "ideal" work/home situations.

A good friend who is an attorney works 2.5 days a week and job shares with a friend.

A physician friend works 3 days per week and has two young children and a part-time nanny.

After a three month maternity leave, a college friend went back to her job as editor of a local magazine. Her husband took off the fourth month to be home with their new baby and when that month is up, she will work 3 days a week.

Another good friend works in marketing research at a large computer company three days a week. She has three young children and a full-time nanny.

My sister Betsy is a nurse and works Monday evenings and every other weekend while her attorney husband, Joe, cares for their three kids.

More and more of our friends have worked out similar arrangements, so that one of the spouses can pursue his or her career interests while minimizing the "day-care" hours for their kids.

As I see it, these friends have a golden egg. They still have the stimulation and self-esteem of a career, yet they have twice as much time with their families as most working parents. But these "ideal" situations are few and far between. It's too bad there are not more of them because they help make happy parents, and happy parents are good parents.

I also believe that a happy worker is a good worker. When Ginny and I owned our own company, we had a predominantly female office. Approximately 40 out of 60 employees were female. I was the first woman in our company to have a baby, so I set the standard. At the time our company was not that large, but we gave six weeks paid maternity leave to all moms. And they could take up to six months unpaid. We gave new dads some paid days off, and they could take unpaid parental leave if they chose.

When one of our managers came to me after having a baby and asked if she could work part time, I said, "We're a women's company. If we can't find a way to work this out, then we're in trouble." So we worked out a part-time schedule for her management position. And you know what? She loved it. She produced and was happy and stayed on with us because of it.

I don't think U.S. corporations fully realize the importance of valuing families. We're far behind other countries in accommodating families in the workforce. In time corporations will be forced to accommodate working parents with more flexible alternatives. It's already beginning to change, but there's a long, long way to go. Over 56% of the U.S. workforce is made up of parents with children under age 17. If corporations want to attract the best and the brightest, chances are that the majority of them will be parents someday. So if U.S. corporations really want to be competitive and quality driven, they *will* find more ways to attract and retain talented parents. Maybe by the time our children are parents, they'll have more flexible career options than we do. If they don't, then our generation will have progressed no further than the generation before us.

But I was dealing with reality. And the reality was that there wasn't an "ideal" career situation for me that would allow me to contribute and accomplish all I wanted to accomplish at home with our kids.

So as I sat there in the airport, I reminded myself that I hadn't made a mistake. I had decided I didn't want to work full time outside the home. For now I was satisfied with my career choice to be at home raising our children. I just had to figure out how to get myself back on track.

My choice had changed my life drastically, and I was having difficulty dealing with how much I missed from my old life. Even though I had sworn off nylons five months before, professing that I would never wear them on a regular basis again, I missed dressing up in "grown-up" clothes, wearing pumps, and feeling I had an adult identity. I missed the challenge and creative outlet of work. I missed the social stimulation of the workplace. And I missed the dual role I used to have as a peer and a comrade with my husband.

It was that day in the airport that I realized these voids were real. And it was that same day that I began my mission to fill these voids so I could be fulfilled and happy in my new role as at-home mom.

My mission isn't complete. I'm still working to fill each of the "voids" in my life. Writing this book is the way I'm trying to fill my creative need. The next four chapters look at each of these voids and how I'm attempting to fill them and empower myself to balance my own needs with those of my family.

CHAPTER FIVE

I Don't Have a Business Card Anymore

I have never been big on business cards. I only handed them out at business meetings when everybody else did. But I always carried them with me. They were tucked away in my wallet just in case I needed to be reminded of who I was. And when somebody did ask me what I did, I always had the option of handing them my card, complete with title and place of employment.

But my new career didn't come with business cards. And when I realized they weren't tucked in my wallet, it was as if I lost a part of myself. A job title had made me feel important. I know, I know. Being a mother and raising children is one of the most important jobs in the world. I kept telling myself that every day. But somehow I just could not fill that

emptiness in my wallet and in myself.

When I started staying home with our kids, I found one of the first things I would ask other at-home parents was what they used to do.

"Have you been at home with your kids since they were born? Where did you used to work?" And off the conversation would go, away from diapers and kids.

I began to realize my true motivation in asking these questions. As our conversation unfolded I would have the opportunity to tell these new acquaintances *what I used to do.* I believed people would value me more because of what I had accomplished outside the home. I needed them to have this information while they were forming a first impression of me. I wanted to scream, "Don't look at me changing this diaper. I used to be somebody with a job title, damn it."

I started dreading going to parties or meeting new people who would ask, "What do you do?" It just didn't sound as *important* to say "homemaker" as it did to say, "I run a small marketing company with my sister." That's why I had stared and stared at the occupation box on the form before I filled in "Homemaker." The word itself made me feel unimportant.

But what really brought it home was when Kelley gave me the Mother's Day card she had made in preschool. She had drawn a picture of me (which was humbling enough) and had written a story that went like this:

> *"My mom has brown hair and blue eyes. She's thirty-two years old. For her work she does laundry, cleans the kitchen and empties the dishwasher. Her favorite food is ice cream. I love my mom."*

I panicked. All she thought I could do is laundry and dishes. Didn't she know what I used to do and who I used to be? What kind of role model was I?

LEARNING TO VALUE MYSELF MORE THAN MY ACCOMPLISHMENTS

I was already struggling to get comfortable with the labels "homemaker" and "mother." I was fighting my instincts to define my accomplishments and contributions in terms of success in the workplace. The way I reacted when I read Kelley's Mother's Day card made me realize I had a long way to go to feel okay about my choice.

I know logically it's not what I do that defines me. We all should know it's who we are more than what we do that gives us our self-worth. But it was hard for me to value myself and my contribution in the role of mother and homemaker when so many of society's messages put value on other roles and contributions. I think this is slowly changing as more and more baby-boomers make choices that put more emphasis on family. It's becoming "acceptable" for both mothers and fathers to have a more active role in raising their kids.

But for me the bottom line was that my job outside the home had given me a label other than "mom." It somehow defined who and what I was outside of my children and my spouse. It gave me the tangible rewards of a career:

Getting a paycheck every two weeks reminds you, "Yes, I did my job. I'm worth something."

Getting a bonus at the end of the year says, "Yes, I met the objectives for the year. I accomplished all I set out to do."

Getting a review at year-end reminds you how you performed and where you need to improve, and perhaps even steers you to some training courses to help you get there.

For me, my work outside the home had been tangible and concrete and measurable. I had a good idea of how I was doing in relation to my goals.

Being at home is intangible and blurry. I usually don't have a clue as to how I'm doing.

Dinnertime is "catch-up time." It's the time when Dave and I check in with each other. He usually has something to report from the office, complete with some concrete accomplishment. "I finished my product plan, and I finally started planning for our trade show next week."

My days are definitely not concrete. They are repetitive. They provide no feedback and little insight on how I'm doing in relation to my goal of raising happy, self-confident kids.

"Well, I picked up the toys in the den five times today. It's hard to tell right now because it's been 45 minutes since the last time I picked up. And I read *Too Much Noise* to Charlie 15 times. Even Kelley's getting sick of it. Kelley cut the Christmas tree out of the *Sesame Street* magazine all by herself, didn't you, Kelley? Oh, and Janie didn't nap all day. She was so fussy that I had to hold her all afternoon. I think she's cutting her upper teeth."

Dave's out working at his rewarding job, and I'm here investing all of my time and energy into my job of raising our kids, with little positive reinforcement. Day in, day out I get up and do my job. But there's no paycheck to remind me I'm doing okay. There's no year-end bonus to say, "Job well done, Kate." On the other hand, there's nobody to fire me if I scream at my kids all day. There's nobody to say, "No bonus for you, kid. You didn't perform to the standards we set for mothers."

And that's part of the problem, there are no standards.

A friend of mine said to me the other day, "Some days I think, here I am giving everything I have to raising my two girls, and I don't have the slightest idea if I'm screwing it up. What if I fail?"

It's really hard to know how you're doing day to day.

I didn't create a workplan at the beginning of the year with measurable goals that get reviewed. My goals change day to day, actually minute to minute, depending on how our kids are doing.

No mentor or boss is observing me and giving me feedback on what I can do to improve. Basically I wing it and try every day to do the best I can. There are some days I think I did pretty well. But there are also many days I know I didn't do so hot.

FOCUSING ON WHO I AM

In light of that, the biggest challenge for me is keeping my self-worth and self-esteem high. My self-worth doesn't get a boost from making a sale or from what I accomplished. It comes from within. It comes from who I am every day with my kids. Am I yelling and nagging, or am I a positive, happy force in their lives? It comes from focusing on my role and career as mother.

I slowly realized that in order to feel good about me and my role at home, I have to believe in it with my whole heart. And it has helped me enormously to take time each morning before I get out of bed to reflect on myself and my role at home. Every morning I wake up and say this prayer before I rise for the day:

God, help me be a happy voice in my children's lives today. It's a privilege to have this time with them. I don't want to hurry my way through these precious years - I want to savor every minute and have fun with our kids.

Help me take this responsibility seriously, but not too seriously. Help me to remember to laugh more and say no less. And most of all, give me the strength I need to be patient when I feel I have no patience left, to listen when my ears are full, and to forgive myself when I blow it. Their very life is a miracle to be treasured and respected. Thanks for giving me the opportunity to help these three children grow.

It helps.

But on many mornings, within 15 minutes of my little prayer, I'm screaming my head off at Charlie to stop whining for more juice. "You've had three cups already and this whining has got to stop!"

Then I take a deep breath, compose myself, and try to figure out why I said no in the first place. I realize I really need to pick my battles, and this little battle over juice definitely isn't worth it.

It's obvious to me, as I look back over the past two years at home with our kids, that I'm the one who has grown the most. It has forced me to look at myself without my business cards in my wallet. And in doing so I've had to find a more honest, true worth that is based on who I am, and not necessarily on what I accomplish and how others view me.

When I look back to when I worked outside the home, I realize my job title had been a shield. Those business cards gave me a false sense of security, like the house that was built on sand. When that job title was washed away, it uncovered things I realized I needed to deal with. Some pretty basic things.

I had to like myself even when my kids did not. I am a pleaser, and pleasing kids is not always easy. And they definitely let me know when they are not pleased.

I had to focus on my role at home and my comfort level with that role rather than my comfort level with how others would perceive me.

I had to learn all over how to like myself without getting "A's," without getting raises, and without getting daily feedback on how I was doing.

It took months of effort and affirmation of myself and my role. I spent time reflecting and journalizing my thoughts as I began to unravel a deeper sense of myself.

A friend of mine told me that in her daughter's elementary school they don't grade the work. Two years ago I would have been astounded. I was so tuned into outside reinforcement that I probably would have thought, "What a crazy concept. Kid's need concrete goals, measurements, and healthy competition to succeed. How else will they improve?"

But now I view it differently. When my friend described the program to me, I expounded with great enthusiasm, "What a wonderful way for children to learn not just to like themselves for what they accomplish, but to like the process of learning and to like who they are. To strive to be the best they can, not for a grade or recognition, but for themselves."

I'm learning that concept first hand at home with our kids, and I'm happier and more in touch with myself than I've been in a long time. I feel now as though my self-worth is built on rock (okay, maybe just wood, but certainly not sand!). And as hard as it is for me to stay "up" day to day, I feel much more able to do that now then when I first started staying home two years ago.

And when I'm up and feeling happy and good about me and about being here with our kids, I can see the difference in the kids. They're happier, too.

When I meet other at-home parents, I've stopped asking quick questions about what they used to do or where they used to work. I wait awhile to ask those questions. I don't want to put them in boxes and affix labels to them, and I don't want other people to do that to me. I have learned to value myself and others, not for what they are, but for who they are. And I really, really like that.

That doesn't mean I don't want to pursue interests and challenges outside of my kids. I definitely do. And it doesn't mean I don't want to hear about other people's professions and careers. I find it intellectually energizing to talk about other people's interests and experiences. But when I do, I'm doing so now with a greater comfort with myself and confidence in my job title as "homemaker" and "mother"...because the bottom line is, that's my new job. And it truly is the most important job in my life.

CHAPTER SIX

Fishing for a New Walter

THE VOID OF HAVING A CHALLENGE

My sister Ginny is truly a visionary. She thinks bigger than life. When we worked together, there was nothing more invigorating than the thrill of the hunt. The challenge of going after the goal that seemed out of reach, hooking it, and then reeling in the catch.

But as soon as we reached the goal, we started looking for the next big fish to catch. Ginny termed our obsession "searching for Walter." The Walter she referred to was the elusive fish Henry Fonda pursued so avidly every summer in the movie, "On Golden Pond."

I like that analogy. For Henry Fonda's character the pursuit of Walter kept him going. The prospect of actually catching Walter got him up and out in the morning. It helped keep him alive.

We all need a Walter, something to continually strive for, to help us feel valid and alive.

When I first started staying home full time, it was like shell shock. It's very difficult to be humming along at an *allegro* tempo one day, and then have to slow down to *polo* the next. The contrast between the high creative energy at work and my days at home was BIG to say the least. In just one day I went from having a list of meaty goals at work to my daily goal at home of trying to get all the kids to nap at the same time.

I don't want to glamorize my career. I did my share of grunt work. But at least every day was different from the one before and full of energy and stimulating people. It was great to feel that my mind was being stretched and challenged for at least a portion of each day.

In contrast, after being at home a couple of months, it started to seem like every day was the same. Kids like routine, and we definitely developed ours. Ours get up at 6:00 like clockwork and want to eat breakfast right away — cereal, juice, and toast. Only once in a great while can I convince them to go out on a limb and try a frozen waffle instead of Cheerios or orange juice instead of apple.

Next we get dressed, pick up our rooms, clean the breakfast dishes, and put in a load of laundry. Then we read books, do some puzzles, and the routine is on track: carpools, preschool, parenting class. Some days it really gets to me. If I have to pick up the toys in the den, empty the dishwasher, and then read *Good Night Moon* just one more time, I'll scream!

It's not that our days at home aren't busy. They're very full. It's just that they are full of the same things day after day. For me, quite honestly, the routine started to get boring and left me feeling like I wanted to explode out of the house and run for miles. And I hate running.

And then one day it came to a head. It had been a long, cold week with more time spent inside than usual. Kelley and I were playing an intense game of Candy Land to pass the hours. I was ahead by a mile, with just one more curve to reach Lost Candy Castle and win. That's when it happened. Kelley picked Queen Frostine on her next turn, and wouldn't you know, I picked Mr. Mint. I was doomed.

"After this, Kel, we'll play again. Whoever wins two games in a row will be the winner, okay?"

"But Mommy, I am the winner already. I got to the Candy Castle first." She was confused and definitely wasn't into the competition concept.

"Yes, you won this game. But we're having a Candy Land contest. The real winner is the one who wins two games in a row. If you win the next game, then you're the contest champion. If I win the next game, we'll play again to see who the champion is. Okay?"

"That's cheating, Mom. I'm the winner. I'm gonna tell Dad you cheated when he gets home from work."

That's when it hit me. I really wanted to win. I mean, I really, really wanted to beat the pants off my four-year-old daughter. I was tired of letting her have all the glory. I wanted another run up the rainbow trail, past Grandma Nutty to the winner's circle. I wanted my moment in the sun, my chance for victory.

The scary part was that my need for a challenge was at the expense of my four-year-old daughter. My attempt to build a little competition into our afternoon game of Candy Land was for me.

The look on her face, and even more, her threat to tattle to Daddy that I cheated, took me down a few notches. This was definitely not a healthy way for me to find my next Walter.

FINDING MY CHALLENGES OUTSIDE THE HOME

I had learned that Candy Land tournaments weren't going to fulfill the void of fishing for a Walter. Not if I wanted to have any self-respect left, anyway.

So I began to force myself to pursue other interests and challenges outside the home. Instead of doing chores or picking up during nap times and evenings, I started to put aside "have tos" and dig into something of interest to me. I started by volunteering on a board for a local youth foundation.

It was the night of my first committee meeting. I watched the clock all afternoon, anxious for my evening out. After dinner, I peeled off my jeans and sweatshirt and donned my only sporty outfit. Notebook in hand and dirty dishes in the sink, I was off.

It was as if a caged animal had been let loose. I took my place at the conference table and stalked the others at the meeting, taking them each in slowly. They went around the table and introduced themselves; their names, what they did, how many kids they had, how long they had been on the committee.

And then it was my turn. I pounced. I started talking and I don't think I could have stopped even if I had wanted to. I monopolized the entire meeting. I was new to the committee, but the way I was interjecting and commenting throughout the evening, you would have thought I was chairman of the board.

As the meeting wound down, so did I. I was smacking my lips and wiping my brow. I had outdone myself. I was finally talked out. And as I shut my mouth and began to listen, I became more embarrassed by the minute.

So I spoke up one more time, "I promise this will be the last time I'll talk for the evening, but I do have to say one more thing. Thanks so much for having me on this committee. I hope I didn't scare you all by how much I talked, it's just that I don't get out much. Three preschoolers at home and all...I mean, I haven't been around this meeting stuff in awhile, and I just got carried away. I'm not normally like this, really. But thanks, this is the greatest!"

They all just smiled and nodded. They knew they had me hooked. Another ex-business-woman let loose from the home-front. Before I knew it, I *was* vice president of the board.

As I began rediscovering my intellect through committees and volunteering, I found that being a career mom at home really was an opportunity for me to get involved in causes I had always cared about and to pursue interests for which I had never had time. Writing is one of them.

Not only has writing this book helped me to focus on how to be a happier mom, but the challenge has been exciting for me. Even if this book is read only by my family and friends, I'll feel as though I've had an outlet for my creativity and thoughts. And I'll feel proud that I finished it. The process of writing it has helped me grow and reach a goal outside my kids. I can't tell you what a difference that makes in my life. It has been critical for me to have something outside the home to keep me going.

STAYING ACTIVE

Once I was recharged, I was on a roll. There was a whole big world out there, and I was bound and determined not to miss it by staying cooped up all winter. In order to stay challenged and creatively stimulated, I knew I had to stay active.

It's easy to start feeling listless and low and, in turn, depressed and repressed. That's especially so here in Minnesota, where winter is almost half the year and it gets dark before 5:00 pm. To help counter that feeling, I make sure we all get outside for fresh air at least once a day, no matter what the weather. Midwinter I have to force myself to load up all three kids in their car seats and trek over to the community pool for a swim, and I consider myself successful if I can pawn that duty off on Dave. But swimming and gymnastics give the kids the opportunity to develop gross motor skills as well as to stay physically energized.

I'm no athlete, but that's been important for me, too. I play in a tennis league every Monday, and I try to get out for a walk or ride the bike two to three times a week. I've found that when I'm energized physically, I have more energy at home to stay stimulated with our kids.

DISCOVERING MY CAREER AT HOME

That brings me to the third and most important way I'm trying to break the doldrums of daily routine at home with kids. I'm trying to focus on my role as caretaker of our three children as my *career.* I try to figure out ways to channel my creativity into making our days full and rewarding—for them, as well as for me.

When I first started staying home, I was like a toddler engaging in parallel play. "You work on coloring this picture while Mommy calls Aunt Maggie." Or, "You play with these Legos while Mommy folds the laundry." It was hard for me to get into the mode of playing *with* the kids.

I've learned. Now I play with the kids, but with a purpose. I don't believe I need to or should play with our kids *all* day. They need to develop skills in playing independently and to learn to enjoy alone time. Plus, I need time to get things done around the house.

However, I truly believe that what motivates our kids at home is getting attention from us, their parents. When my kids weren't getting enough attention from me at home all day, they started acting out in attention-getting behaviors: fighting, hitting, whining. Here's the scenario:

"Mom," Kelley whines, "Will you read me this book?"

"No," Charlie counters, "You read me dis book."

"In a minute, guys. Just let me finish cleaning up these lunch dishes. Why don't you look at the pictures together for a little bit?"

Charlie grabs the book out of Kelley's hand. Kelley hits Charlie and screams, "GIVE IT BACK." Charlie screams and bites. Both kids are screaming and crying.

"OKAY. THAT'S ENOUGH! TIME FOR NAPS. UP WE GO!" I'm screaming, they're screaming, we're all screaming, and we all feel frustrated and crabby as hell.

When my kids weren't getting enough of my time, this attention-getting behavior became a pattern. I hated it, and I hated the way I was responding to their behavior. A negative tone had been established.

Okay, so how could I apply my problem-solving skills from work to creatively change our pattern? After all, I had been successful in business, so I should be able to tackle this.

I had identified the cause of their behavior, attention getting. So I decided to test new ways to involve the kids in what I was doing to help resolve the situation. Maybe it wasn't the same "thrill" as selling a big client, but it was my new "Walter," and I started getting into it.

When I had chores to do around the house, I'd involve them. Instead of saying, "Kelley, you and Charlie read in here together while I do the dishes" and then waiting for the yelling to ensue, I'd say, "Let's scrub the lunch dishes and you guys put them in the dishwasher for me," or "Let's wash the kitchen floor and then we'll play in the basement." I'd give Kelley (age 4) and

Charlie (age 2) each a small bucket of Ivory soap suds and a sponge and let them go at it. I'd follow with my bucket and mop up their suds. Sometimes I'd even get Janie (9 months) down from her highchair and let her splash around.

When I folded laundry, they did it right along with me. They were not the neat stacks our nanny used to fold, but you could see the pride and self-esteem building in the kids as they were allowed to "help."

But more than that, we'd have fun while we did it, singing silly songs and pretending. Sometimes, I'd be Cinderella and they'd be the wicked stepsisters telling me to "mop it up." Other times they'd be the mom and dad and I'd be the baby. (As hard as I may try, I can never seem to land the starring roles.)

No matter, they were transforming into much, much happier children because I was engaging them in what I was doing. And in turn, I became much more fulfilled because I was having fun interacting with my kids.

As I spent more time involved with the kids, their creativity and imagination were contagious. I discovered easy ways to break up our routine and keep the kids excited and interested day to day. Things that were as elementary as having backwards day and eating pizza for breakfast and cereal for dinner, or wearing our PJ's all day and putting on clothes to wear to bed. The littlest change in our schedule became a treat and made our day more fun. Simply setting up lunch in a tent in the basement would keep us entertained for hours.

And it's always a sure bet to play with water: washing dishes or dolls in the sink, filling up squirt guns and shooting them in the shower, or when I'm really at wits end, simply plunking them all in the bathtub midday with pots and pans. They love it.

That doesn't mean I'm constantly bouncing around the house and entertaining the kids. It takes a lot of energy to engage three kids every day, and some days, I'm just too tired. But after getting into my creative mode for a few months, I also mastered the art of passively engaging the kids. I call it "couch parenting." It's what I resort to mid-afternoon when I need a 10-minute power nap:

I lay face down on a pillow and become a mountain. The kids climb up my legs to my back and jump off. I simply close my eyes and get a great back rub with their feet.

We play sick Mommy. I lay on the couch and they are the team of doctors and nurses. Doctor kits in hand, they poke and prod me with the play thermometer and stethoscope, make me pretend tea and toast, and I take a 10 minute cat nap.

We play school. I sit in the armchair in the principal's office and watch while they take turns being teacher and student.

The list is endless. But I've found it much more effective than simply saying, "Watch this video while I take a rest." That was simply an invitation for them to fight. My couch parenting keeps the focus and attention on them with minimal energy or output from me.

As we march around the house in a "parade" putting away laundry I often think how mortified I'd be if my friends could see the levels I stoop to entertain the kids. Actually, the scary thing is that I've found that it entertains me the most.

But I find the more I "engage" myself with the kids, the happier they are and the happier I am. We have lots of tea parties, build lots of forts, and basically have lots of fun. And I truly feel more creative and challenged trying to simultaneously keep a 4- and 2-year-old and a 9-month-old stimulated than many times when I worked outside the home.

Part of it is my attitude shift, too. I am trying to minimize the parallel play with my kids ("you do this while I do that") and trying to either find more ways to include them in what I'm doing or really get into what they're doing. I'm hopeful that by doing so I will make them feel loved and special and self-worthy. I know it's helping me feel a whole lot better about the time I spend with them at home.

PLANNING AND ORGANIZING MY DAYS

I had Walter on the line. "Engaging" the kids was definitely giving them more focus and attention, but with three young children under age five, I still felt like I was a pinball bouncing willy nilly between the needs of each child. In order to reel in this lunker, I needed some method to my madness.

So upon the recommendation of a friend, I went to her community center to hear a speaker on goal setting. Okay, I'll be honest, I said I'd go because it was a great excuse to put on those dusty pumps again and go out for the evening. Perhaps we'd stop for coffee and pie after the workshop. But I actually was taken in by the speaker. It was as if I were Moses, and God was speaking to me through a burning bush. I knew that the keynote speaker was looking right at me with every point she made. Through the course of her presentation, I felt like Rocky "getting strong now."

Just because my career was at home with kids, I was not precluded from goal setting. Yes, I could reach for loftier goals than getting all three kids to nap at the same time each day. I could set and reach goals in my career as mother.

So as I walked out of the presentation that night, I was first in line to buy one of the planning/goal calendars that were for sale for $39.99. No wonder the workshop was free.

The calendar is really nothing more than a daily planner that basically organizes your life. I was finally going to give some directed thought at how to structure our days at home. I began by talking with Dave. That night, in fact, as soon as I got home.

"Okay, honey, I want to do this goal setting thing together and set goals for our family. We are supposed to base them on our values. What do you think our values are?" I laid this on him at 9:30 pm before we hopped into bed.

"Kate, is this going to be like the family meeting program you were on last year when Kelley was only three and Charlie was one." He was a skeptic. Our first meetings had been very humorous, and I had resorted to bribing the kids with M&M's the entire half-hour just to keep them at the table.

"Hey, those family meetings got better as they got older. And no, this is not a kick. This is for me. For us." And I repeated what the speaker had said at the presentation, and how I thought goal setting at home would really help me be a better mother day in and out. So, we started listing our values and prioritizing them. We then took each value and made a list of corresponding goals that reinforced the value.

It may sound a little heady, but it was really just a matter of thinking it through and writing it down. For example, our top value was easy...cherishing our family. We then made a list of corresponding goals that supported valuing family. A couple of the biggest goals were (1) to build self-esteem and confidence in our kids, and (2) to teach them life skills like sharing, honesty, good communication, respect for themselves and others.

The hard part came when we tried to whittle these lofty goals into daily tasks with kids. Obviously self-esteem building had always been a goal, but was there something I could plan to do each day that would further that goal at home? Quit screaming at them was obvious, but what else?

After talking it through, we figured it might help build each child's self-esteem to know that I took the time to do something one-on-one with them each day. Something that was important to them. And in the process of doing an activity with them, I could try to help them master a new task that would further build self-esteem. On the days that Dave was home early and on weekends, he would do the same.

My one-on-one times with the kids aren't elaborate or involved, but the difference has been that I've made them a priority and scheduled them on my to-do list, right along with the lists of phone-calls, errands, lessons, play-dates, and household chores I need to do. It helps remind me throughout the day what is really important about staying home, and I'm hoping it helps us reach the goal of building their self-esteem.

I discovered that it wasn't so much what we did, it was that I took the time every day to spend it with each child alone, dedicating my attention and my self to each child as an individual.

Next came our goal of how to build life skills and integrity for our three young children. We thought one way to reach that goal would be to plan at least one group activity a day that we did together at home or on an outing. My hope was that we'd set "guidelines" together as a family about treating each other with respect, being honest, learning to apologize and forgive when problems occur. Stuff we had always worked on anyway, but by writing it down and thinking it through together, we would hopefully all feel a part of the family "rules."

When I looked at the list of guidelines, it hit me that these rules went for me, too. "Listen to others. Help out when asked." Janie's first words had been "Just a minute," and it made me think about how infrequently I was following these guidelines myself. Our list helped me ponder the significance of what I was doing at home, and it made me realize the importance of being consistent. And even more so, it reinforced that when talking to Dave or the kids, I had to set a healthy example.

Sometimes our family activities help us reach our goals, and sometimes they totally bomb. Not too long after we started on our daily group activities, we planned a family outing to cut down our Christmas tree. It was a beautiful, sunny December afternoon, about 30 degrees.

We packed up a picnic, along with snowsuits, boots, and mittens and headed an hour north to the tree farm. Singing Christmas carols in the car, I thought to myself, "This is what it's all about."

But the car ride started getting long, and Charlie had to go to the bathroom. Kelley spilled her pop all over Janie, and to top it off, the clouds were sweeping toward us. By the time we got to the tree farm, a cold front had moved in and it was 4 degrees and cloudy. The kids were tired, cold, and hungry. They whined for us to carry them the entire time, and out of the fifteen minutes we were actually out of the car, I think that at least one of the three kids was always crying.

I have to admit, I was getting a little ornery myself. Dave was determined to find the perfect tree, and although I didn't really like the only decent tree we had found, I finally turned to him and snapped, "I'm freezing. If I can't feel my toes, either can the kids. Just cut down this one. It'll be fine. I'll take the kids and wait in the car."

So for twenty-five minutes we made funny faces on the car window as we watched Daddy cut down our Christmas tree and tie it on top of the car. So much for working together. The hour car-ride back was tense. No carols, no stories, just whining. By the time we got home, Dave was so glad to be there, he sped up the driveway and into the garage...the tree still on top of the car.

But by the next night when we listened to carols, whipped up some hot cocoa, and got out decorations for our new tree, the kids were angelic. It was a cozy scene, you might say right out of Norman Rockwell. Although over half the branches were gone from one side of the tree, we just pushed it up that much closer to the wall and donned it our "space-saver" tree. The mood was down-right festive, and our family activity was a success. Some days it just works!

I attempt not to get too cerebral about this whole process. I try to temper all of this organization with spontaneity. I don't want to get so regimented that I run an army brigade. If a friend calls in the morning and invites us over, I'll throw my planning out the window until the next day. It just gives me comfort to know that I'm not waking up with a blank slate, and I don't have to wing it like I did those first months at home. By treating my role at home more like a career, and by planning out my day the way any person would at a job, I have found that I can work toward long-term goals and values. I am parenting with a purpose and a direction, and it has certainly helped give a method to my madness by keeping the kids on the top of my priority list each and every day.

FISHING IN THE QUIET WATERS

Making the kids a priority is something I inherited. As I set out upon the task of raising our kids at home and making their growth and self-esteem our goal, I've also reflected on my own childhood. I am in awe of how my parents raised me and my three sisters. They are my greatest role models. My dad was the one who thought we were all "exceptional." As Barbara Kingsolver wrote in *Beantrees*, no matter what we did, he always made us feel like "it was the moon (we) just hung up in the sky and plugged in all the stars." If I can make our kids feel that special, I'll have caught one big "Walter."

My mom is one of those people who always made the simplest thing fun. She always made me feel loved, as if what I had to say was of the utmost importance. She was and still is a great listener. My friends sometimes stopped by more to talk with her than to see me! If I can be that constant source of love and listening at home with our kids every day, then I will have reeled in my "Walter."

I remember telling my mom once about wanting big accomplishments in my life. I wanted to conquer great and important challenges. She said to me, "Kate, only a few people in the world make a great big splash. And yes, their splash is seen and heard by everyone. But don't forget there are many people out there every day making little waves. And if your little wave touches just one or two other waves and makes those people's lives just a little bit better, and they in turn do the same — wow, what a great world this will be."

I think of those words often now that I'm home with the kids, and I feel as if I've learned their true meaning. The Walters I'm going after aren't the large-mouth bass that I can mount or for which I'll win a trophy. They're definitely still out there, but they're not in the great, active swells or in the fast-moving waters.

I'm fishing off to the side now, in the mellow streams and in the little waves. Dave is right there by my side (baiting my hook and taking off the fish!), and our kids are the ones who are casting and reeling over and over again. It's the process that's important. Doing it together as a family. We may not catch anything for weeks, but we're all standing on the shore, doing it together. And I'm proud to say I'm learning to be very, very happy with that.

CHAPTER SEVEN

Nobody's Home Around Here

THE WAY I PICTURED IT

I grew up in Park Ridge, Illinois, a middle-class suburb outside Chicago. Our neighborhood was made up of big old houses on tree-lined streets. After walking home from Roosevelt Elementary School, I would have a snack of two cookies and a glass of milk, and my sisters and I would share the day's events with our mom. Then we'd change into playclothes and run outside to frolic with all the other kids in the neighborhood.

Around 5:45 we'd walk the four blocks uptown, past the red-brick city hall and the sweet smells of the local bakery, to the train station to meet Dad. I often think what a great

sight that must have been for him, to get off the train after a long day at the office and see his little girls waiting to walk him home for dinner.

I also realize it was a great way for Mom to get dinner ready without four daughters underfoot.

Our town was not unlike many towns in which baby-boomers of the '50s and '60s grew up. Almost everybody's dad worked, and almost everybody's mom was home with the kids, and lots of kids at that! We'd play outside in the neighborhood without a worry. It was a great childhood, carefree and dreamy!

Even before I started staying home full time, I realized that the neighborhoods of my youth were a thing of the past. Crime and working parents had changed that long before I left my job.

Yet tucked back in the corner of my mind was the fantasy that life at home for me would be like life at home had been for my mother. Lots of friends from down the street bopping in for coffee. Kids playing in the yard while we shared the concerns of the world and discussed the latest challenges of raising our children.

How it really was for me...isolated

But my vision was a far cry from what my life at home was like, at first anyway. Prior to closing up my briefcase I had been so busy, between working and raising a family, I hadn't had time to tap into my community. We rarely socialized, and when we did, we spent it with family or old friends. As a result, we hadn't built a network in our neighborhood and community. In addition, our community is a growing suburb and a product of the '70s and '80s — no sidewalks, no "uptown" shopping area where everybody goes, and most of all, nobody home.

Over half the families who have young children have parents who both work. So neither they nor their kids were around on weekdays. The families who did have a parent at home never seemed to be around. I'd see their cars coming and going and coming and going, and I was sure they were all going to play groups without me.

And all the while I was home, isolated in my house, with my two kids and a third one on the way. I was lonely!

So out of desperation for a little adult interaction, I did what I swore I wouldn't. I tuned back into *All My Children*. On my last maternity leave I had gotten so addicted to my soap that I found myself going to extremes just to be home by noon. It got so bad that I even dreamt about Tad Martin. So I swore to myself when I started staying home that I would not go down that sudsy path again. But there I was, rushing the kids through lunch and up to naps, so I could click on ABC.

As much as *All My Children* was a welcome hour in my slow days, I needed more. So to jump start our days at home, I, too, started to come and go and come and go. First it was swimming at the local pool. Then it was church choir. Next gymnastics. It didn't take me long to figure out where all the other at-home parents were. They were busy driving their kids to gym, swimming lessons, skating lessons, ballet, computer class, and the list goes on. It's amazing kids have time to just be kids anymore.

But after gymnastics and swimming were over, I'd return home to the quiet streets and neighborhood.

The hub-hub at kids gymnastics could not replace the social stimulation I used to get at work, the camaraderie that was built from working with others on a common goal. At work I had built close friendships and filled my social quota each day by chatting in the halls, laughing with a co-worker over something that happened at home, or taking time before a meeting to share a critique of the latest movie release, last week's *Northern Exposure* episode, or the president's speech the night before.

After the first couple of lonely weeks at home, the phone became my life line. I found myself picking up the phone during the kids' naptime to call Dave for a daily dose of adult conversation and idle chit-chat, something I had never had the need to do when I had been at the office.

"Hi," I'd say.

"Hi, what's up?" Many times he sounded rushed or had someone in his office.

"Just wondering what time you thought you'd be home."

"Regular time. I'll probably leave here about quarter to six."

"Oh."

"Anything else? How're the kids? How are Janie's teeth today?"

"They're fine. Her teeth are better. I'm just trying to decide whether to make chicken or spaghetti for dinner. What do you feel like?"

"Either one. Whatever's easiest. Listen, Kate, Larry just walked in. I gotta go. I'll talk to you later, okay?"

"Fine. Sorry to bother you." I'd hang up the phone with a slight bang to relieve my aggravation.

It was bad enough that "what to make for dinner" was a major decision in my day, but even more pitiful was the fact that I was calling Dave at work about it.

After hanging up the phone I thought, "I've got to get a life. I'm living an episode from a *Dick Van Dyke Show* rerun."

It's not as though I didn't have friends who were home with kids, too. My sister Betsy has three kids almost the same ages as ours. We love to get together, but she lives a half hour away, and we're both tied to preschool and carpool schedules. Most of my other friends live far enough away that I'm not about to get the kids in the car and drive over to just "stop by," especially in the middle of winter when I have to get them dressed in their snow-suits and boots.

I'd try to arrange "play-dates" — a '90s phenomenon — to make it worth while to pack up the car and drive over for a visit. But with nap times, feedings, and school schedules, it was hard to find a time that was right for everyone. So most days I just stayed home and felt isolated and alone. By the time Dave walked in the door, I was ready to talk his ear off.

"You just don't know what it's like. I haven't spoken to one other adult all day. I tried to talk to Kate Triggs on the phone, but Charlie was screaming and I had to hang up. I swear these kids are trying to sabotage any attempt I have at a social outlet. Every time I get on the phone, they scream for candy. And worse, I find myself shoving it in their mouths just to finish a 5-minute conversation. I had to stretch the phone cord and lock myself in the bathroom so I could talk to the plumber about the leaking sink. With all the screams he heard in the background, it's no wonder he said he couldn't help me. He was probably scared to set foot in this house. It's a nightmare."

Dave would try to throw me a bone and empathize, which would somehow just infuriate me more.

"It's not the same for you at all," I'd argue. "You have lots of adult conversations with your co-workers. You shoot the breeze with your buddies at work, plus you get to go out to lunch all the time. I literally haven't spoken to anybody but these kids. I'm going crazy."

PUTTING MYSELF OUT THERE

I knew that the answer to my isolation was to make new friends in the community and in the same schools and programs as our kids. But that's easier said than done. It was the first time in my life that I can remember actually having to make a conscious effort to make friends. Before staying home with the kids, I cultivated friendships through what I did and with whom I did it. Through work, college, high school. Over time, the people with whom I shared these experiences became friends. It just kind of happened.

Now it was up to me and nobody else to make it happen. And being home in my house with preschoolers all day, it was clear that it was not going to be easy. So I began my "new friend" campaign with the goal of meeting other parents in the area with interests in common with mine.

Whenever I'd pack up the kids and set out in the family van, I was in pursuit of adult interaction. It was a desperate picture of myself that I wasn't proud of.

When I'd pick up Kelley at preschool, I'd chat with the other parents. At church, when I'd pick up Charlie and Janie in the nursery, I would linger and make pleasant conversation. At the grocery store I'd turn to a friendly face and inquire, "How do your kids like these Dunkaroos?"

After my outings I'd return home somewhat bolstered by the social stimulation, only to realize that I had from noon to six with no prospect of talking to another adult.

It didn't take me long to discover that occasional chatting over kids' heads while putting on jackets and boots wasn't enough to form lasting bonds.

I had to make myself vulnerable. I had to pick up the phone and call people I'd met just a couple of times and invite them over. I felt like I was back in junior high school.

"What if they don't want to come over?" I asked Dave. This whole mom-bonding thing was new territory for me. But my junior high insecurities subsided quickly when I found out most other moms were in the same boat as I was and they welcomed the invitation.

One of the best ways I met other moms with common interests was through ECFE, our community's Early Childhood Family Education program. This program saved me. It gave me an opportunity to gather with other parents who have kids about the same age as mine. In our community program, classes start with 45 minutes devoted to parent/child interaction time with age-appropriate activities (painting, sand and water tables, etc. — things I rarely do at home). We spend the next 45 minutes in a separate "parenting time," while the kids are supervised by a licensed early childhood teacher in a different room. The discussion time with other parents who have kids the same age as mine was priceless. We'd share ideas on potty-training, discipline, pacifiers. Some of the most effective techniques I now use with my children are actually ideas that other parents have had in these classes.

ECFE is really our generation's structured version of our mothers' coffee klatsch, but with much more information available than our parents ever had. And in the process, I've built friendships with other parents and their kids.

ECFE meets once a week, and it's something I really look forward to. Unfortunately, Minnesota is one of the few states where this is a state- and community-funded program. I believe so much in this program, and the value of early childhood education as a preventive tool for many social problems, that I decided to get more involved. I joined the Advisory Board for our local ECFE program. Working with other volunteers on the board has been a great way to get to know people and start forming friendships. Just like at work, I built friendships over time through my common interests with these other moms.

I've also joined the board of another company dedicated to building self-esteem in youths. The result is that I don't feel so isolated. At the same time, I feel as though I'm contributing something to causes I truly care about.

The age-old proverb, "You reap what you sow," has definitely proven true for me. Once I put myself out there and got involved in programs, I got so much more in return.

BROADENING MY SOCIAL ARENA

Even though I was feeling pleased with the success of my "new friend" campaign, I was fearful my mind was turning to mush. It seemed almost all of my social activities centered around kids.

Then one day I spent almost an hour on the phone with a friend. I wasted two-thirds of my kids' naptime deeply engrossed in a conversation dissecting and analyzing which kids we liked best in the *KidSong Video Collection*. After hanging up the phone, it hit me. It had happened. I had become a one-dimensional mother who could talk about nothing other than child-related and home-related issues. I was fearful that I'd be as dull as a door nail in no time.

My fear was confirmed the next week when I was talking with two of my sisters. "What's new?" they asked.

I always hate that question because it doesn't seem like there's ever much that is new. I paused and finally thought of something non-kid related to add. I said enthusiastically, "Well, Dave and I were in Sears yesterday looking at dishwashers. They make the neatest dishwashers now, so modern, with little computers in them. And they're so quiet!"

Utter silence. It was as if E.F. Hutton had spoken.

Finally Ginny broke the baffled silence. "No! Really, Kate? This is enthralling. Tell us more."

We burst out laughing. My sister Betsy laughed the loudest because she confessed that she had actually started to find the conversation quite stimulating. We decided unanimously that we all definitely needed to get out more.

A good friend who sympathized with my fear invited me to join a book club with some of her friends. I jumped right in. We read great books that I'd otherwise never get around to reading, and we meet once a month at different members' homes for lots of great conversation. The thing I like best about it is that we don't talk about kids. Fewer than half of us have kids, and those of us who do are so happy to be out for a night, it's the last thing we want to talk about.

I also make a point of having "Girls Night Out" with my sisters or different groups of friends at least twice a month while Dave is at home in the evening.

The more involved I've gotten, the more opportunities there are to get involved. Between committee meetings for ECFE, volunteer projects that I work on from home, coordinating the church nursery, meetings to work on this book and get it printed, my book club monthly meetings, community events, and get-togethers with friends, I am getting out much more, meeting lots of new people, and in turn, feeling a lot less lonely.

COMING FULL CIRCLE

As I've made new friends over the past two years and broadened my outside interests, I try not to forget how it was for me when I first started staying home and how intimidating it was to join mom/kid activities. I remember the first time I took Kelley to Open Gym. Our nanny had been taking her until I started to stay home. I wasn't quite sure who was who. Many of the moms stood in their own little groups and talked to each other. Hardly any of them came up to me and made an overture. I remember trying to strike up a few conversations, but they fizzled. The other parents had an energy and interest level when they talked to each other. They had a history and a group dynamic that had already been built.

It was uncomfortable for me at first, but I'm glad I kept on going. In time, I started recognizing faces and getting to know some of the parents. And now, remembering my early experiences, I make an effort in the classes I go to now. I look for the new faces, then go over and introduce myself and start to chat.

I think those are the little waves my mom was talking about.

CHAPTER EIGHT

Equal Partners, or Husband and Wife?

Dave and I have a very "'90s" marriage. Okay, I didn't keep my maiden name when we got married, but I did use it as my middle name. When we started out almost nine years ago, Dave and I discussed children. We both loved the thought of big families and figured we'd have six kids. With three young ones under age five, that's definitely changed.

Both of us were very career minded and agreed that we'd both still work after having children. We figured we could balance our full-time careers and parenthood. Obviously, that's changed, too. Thank God we're both flexible.

Dave has always been supportive of my career. Starting a business takes endless hours of work and without a lot of

payback in the beginning. In those early years starting out in our folks' basement, Ginny and I burned the candle at both ends. Dave and I had bought a small house, had a car payment, plus college loans. Because I wasn't contributing to the family income, the financial burdens were all on him. They were hard, lean years, and Dave was patient and understanding. We were lucky that eventually our business flourished, and our many hours of hard work more than paid off in the long run. But either way, Dave's the kind of life-partner who would have been standing there ready to support me whatever the outcome.

Dave was proud of my business success, and after those early years, we both got quite used to having a dual income. But, along with kids came increased stress with both of us working. When our option of part-time schedules at our current jobs didn't pan out, the obvious solution was for me to stay home with the kids. And Dave was behind me all the way. In fact, if he could keep his full benefits and work four days a week, he would do it. He, too, is a strong proponent of finding balance between work and parenthood. We try to help each other find that balance.

But neither of us could have predicted how the transition from working mom to stay-at-home mom would knock our marriage off-balance.

DIS-EQUILIBRIUM IN OUR MARRIAGE?

Dave and I had always been equal partners in our marriage. Sure,

I did more of the dishes and cooking and he did more garbage and lawns, but it all seemed to even out. Dave would even argue that he pulled more than his half the weight around the house. And that might have been true. He came from a family of four boys, and I thank his mother daily for teaching them the responsibilities of the home. Dave started doing his own laundry when he was 13. He hates the way I iron, so he won't even let me near his shirts. It's great!

But once I started staying home full time, I felt less like a partner and more like a wife. And I will freely admit that the resulting crisis was of my own making.

The first change I saw was my transformation into Hazel herself. I'm not a cleaner, but I felt like I was forever picking up around the house. Things that never bothered me before started driving me crazy. Messy drawers, stacks of papers to be filed. So I'd get into my "white tornado" mode and get everything organized and picked up.

I was forever making excuses to Kelley when she found her latest drawing in the wastebasket. "I guess that must have accidentally fallen in the garbage can, hon. Here, I'll just wipe off the ketchup splat and it'll be as good as new."

Before I left to go out, I'd have to wash all the dishes and scrub the sink. There was something unsettling about coming home to a messy kitchen.

I was constantly picking up around Dave and the kids. It was driving me crazy. It was driving Dave crazy. One day I realized how bad it had really gotten.

Dave was searching through all the closets, pulling things out, pushing couches aside.

"What are you looking for?" I asked in a cocky voice that reeked with "just ask me." I prided myself that despite the piles, I could locate anything in the house within seconds.

"My dry-cleaning from my business trip last week. It was in a green plastic bag from the hotel. I was sure I left it in the closet."

Dave looked some more. Frustrated, he asked me again, "Are you sure you didn't see it? It was dark green. It looked almost like a trash bag."

"I haven't seen it." Again that cocky "I know where everything is" voice.

"Kate, you had to see it. It was a huge green bag sitting in the middle of our closet for three days."

I panicked. "Oh, *that* bag. That big, big trash bag."

"Yep. But it wasn't a trash bag. It was a hotel dry-cleaning bag," he said hopefully. "So, where did you put it?"

"I can't believe this. You should have told me what it was. I thought it was trash. I was sure you had finally sorted out those stacks of papers and clothes you always said you'd get to...I mean it looked just like garbage. It's long gone. I put it out on garbage day."

All Dave's office clothes, shirts, ties, two suits, a big percentage of his hard-earned work wardrobe, off to the dump. All out of my compulsive need to control our living space.

I hadn't even looked in the bag. It had been in the way, and I needed it out of the way. It was as simple as that. Was I becoming compulsive? I never was this anal retentive before staying home.

Dave tried to get me to relax, to let it go. He'd help me with the house chores on the weekend. But I couldn't deal with the disorganization and mess three preschoolers can make everyday. Straightening it out gave me instant gratification. It made me feel in control when my life seemed out of control.

I needed control, like I used to have at the office. But now the house was my office, and I was home all the time. I needed to function and feel as if I had control of my space. So, even after throwing Dave's clothes out as trash, I continued to pick up the den toys five times a day instead of waiting till after the kids had gone to bed. It kept me from tripping over toys and breaking my neck. But more than that, it helped keep me sane.

Picking up, wiping down, putting away. I hated the mundane feeling it created. Every day the list was the same: laundry, emptying the dishwasher, making the beds. It made me feel so "wife-like," and it was boring and repetitive. It was maintenance work, and nobody ever recognized maintenance work. Dave could mow the lawn or trim the trees or paint the house, and you could see the difference. My routine jobs just kept our house running status quo. Nobody would ever walk in and tell me how great it was that I did three loads of laundry a day.

As I got more organized, I also started cooking more and planning meals. I started making shopping lists and recipe cards and cooking dinner almost nightly. Believe me, this was a big change. When we both worked, Dave and I would walk in the door and figure out who would make dinner and what we'd have, and then we'd get to it. No planning.

Not now, though. I started having dinner ready at six, and the very few times Dave wasn't home on time, I was put out. This was my creation for the day, my tangible contribution to the family system, so everyone better eat it and they better like it.

"You hated it, didn't you? You barely ate the chicken." I asked Dave insecurely one night as he picked at his dinner of chicken marinara that I had slaved over during naptime.

"I had a late lunch with Norm. I'm not really hungry."

I thought I would blow. "Well, a late lunch, how nice. It might have been nice if you could have let me know. I mean, how hard's a phone call?" I dumped his plate in the sink with a huff.

It was like an old movie and my worst nightmare combined. Dave kind of looked at me as if to say, "I never pictured it being like this." Neither had I.

The truth is that Dave never expected me to cook dinner, let alone chicken marinara. He's happy to fix soup and sandwiches for us. He's happy to help clean and pick up. He's happy to watch the kids when he's home so I can have a break. He's happy to do almost any of the household stuff, especially if I'm at my wits end. Which I was.

But during my first year at home, I just automatically assumed all these domestic chores myself. Yes, I started to resent them, but I couldn't stop myself.

Looking back at the situation, I realize that I must have felt guilty for not "producing," for not contributing in a real way to the family income. It was all tied to not valuing my role at home as a real "career." If I was home all day, then by God, I better have something to show for it. And kids moved too slowly to produce instant gratification. They didn't give me results every day. And I needed results.

So to get results I became compulsive around the house doing things I hated. In turn, I became resentful and bitter and I felt like I was turning into everything I never wanted to be.

I WANTED FREEDOM BACK

Truth to tell, it wasn't only the chores that bothered me. It was being tied to the house. I was resentful of Dave's freedom. His ability to go out to fun places for lunch. His freedom to go to work at 6:00 am and leave by 2:30 pm in the summer and get in 18 holes of golf and still be home for family dinner. His business trips where he got to be alone on a plane for three hours. I mean, he could actually read an entire book. And after a night on the road, he'd retire to his cozy hotel room, order room service, and get 8 hours of uninterrupted sleep. That is unless he stayed up late watching ESPN. But there was no getting up to soothe a child's bad dream or get one of the kids a drink of water.

Yep, I was downright jealous.

I knew the freedom and flexibility working outside the home could bring. I had it for the first two and a half years we had kids. And I wanted it back. When I had been working, it was a snap to run out at lunch and have time with a friend without getting a babysitter. If the kids needed socks and I needed new underwear, it was no problem. I'd run to Dayton's on a break without the worry of three kids hiding under the clothing racks and running down the escalators. If I had a list of personal phone calls to get out of the way, I'd simply dial away in the quiet of my office without kids screaming the minute I picked up the receiver. It used to be so easy to stop at the grocery store on my way home from work. Now it was a three-ring circus with each kid wanting this and that and climbing out of the cart and opening food as quickly as I threw it into the basket.

Okay, everything is relative and I knew that in actuality I had it pretty darn good. Healthy kids. Loving husband. Food on the table every night. Nice house. The family van. My Catholic guilt starting whispering in my ear, "You have no right to be malcontent, honey. You've got it pretty darn good."

But it all comes back to things being relative, to comparing my flexibility - or lack thereof - with Dave's. I was at home and could see how much freedom and flexibility he had. And I knew I had lost mine. And the bottom line was that it set me off.

The more I stewed about it, the more tied-down I felt. And by the time Dave walked in the door at night, I was crabby and tired. And I was also feeling guilty for acting that way. But the more I tried to stop, the worse it got. It was like a moth drawn to a flame.

I didn't know what the answer was. I wanted to be home with the kids, but I didn't want to spend these precious years resenting my husband and ending up with no marriage.

Then came the breaking point. Golf.

When I married Dave I knew he was a die-hard golfer, which was no big deal before we had kids. We had agreed early in our marriage that a good time for him to play golf was Saturday mornings. I have to admit I counted on it not being every Saturday morning, what with bad weather and summer activities. But God knows, Dave is such a die-hard golfer, he was out there every Saturday morning come rain, cold, or typhoon.

Saturday was the one morning in the week when I didn't have to get up and go through the breakfast and get-everyone-dressed routine all by myself. Or at least I thought I shouldn't have to. Sunday was no good because we were always in a rush to get to church. I hadn't realized how much it would bother me when Dave shot out the door early and took my free Saturday morning with him. If I'd been a crab before, now I was a certified lobster. Dave would ask me what was wrong, and it just made me madder that he couldn't see. It was plain as day to me.

The breaking point arrived midway through last summer . The kids had gotten the stomach flu for a week and a half. We were quarantined in our house, and with one of the three kids running to the bathroom every hour, there was no hope of a babysitter. I had been mopping up throw-up and wiping bottoms for ten days. I was tied to the house and had no relief. And, when the weekend finally arrived, Dave was committed to a golf tournament. He had planned this event early in the spring and had been looking forward to it all summer. I knew he couldn't get out of it. But as hard as I tried, I couldn't hold up my martyr syndrome anymore.

"I know I haven't been talking to you lately and when I have, I've been a crab. I've tried to get past this, but I can't. I'm resentful of you and your flexibility. You go to work each day and get a change of scenery and challenge. You go out to lunch. You sit and read the newspaper over coffee when you get to work. You go to trade shows in great cities and talk to real people. AND most of all you get free time all to yourself whenever you golf. I know you work hard and need your breaks, too, but I'm jealous of what you have and I don't. You seem to work it all out so that on top of it all, you're home with the kids, too, playing the part of 'Mister Wonderful Dad.' If I have to hear how great you are from my friends one more time, I'll scream."

Among Dave's other sterling traits, he truly values what I contribute at home with the kids. He has had them to himself numerous evenings and weekends when I've needed a break. I just wish sometimes he could have them for two weeks straight to understand what it's like being at home day in and day out.

"Why don't you do more for yourself, Kate. Get a babysitter during the day a couple of times a week and go to lunch with a friend, or get more involved in your volunteer work, or just have time alone. You need that. No wonder you're going crazy. I couldn't do what you do without some time to myself. I'm happy to watch the kids in the evenings so you can get out."

"By the time dinner's through, I'm dog tired. I don't feel like going out for my own time at 7:30 pm. Plus, it's our only chance at time together. And getting a babysitter is not that easy. Where do you find a good babysitter for just a few hours a week? And the kids hate those drop-off places, plus Janie's too little to go to them. It's not like I can just pick up and leave. And if I use a sitting service, it's super expensive and they send someone different every time. Last time I was desperate I called one. They sent a total stranger. I didn't know her; the kids didn't know her. They were screaming at the door as I pulled out of the driveway. I felt worse than when I left for work everyday. At least they knew and loved Laurie. It was so stressful for me that day, I couldn't enjoy my time away. It wasn't even worth it. Plus, who am I going to do something with even if I could get a babysitter? It's not like my friends can just pick up and leave their kids or jobs either. When we get together, it's always with kids. Maybe I should get a part-time job. I'll work at a local retail shop or waitress again."

"Oh, you'd love that, Kate. If somebody asked you to hang something on a rack, you'd probably tell them to do it themselves."

"That is not true. I'd be glad to have someone to talk to and to get out of the house for a little bit. Plus I would like to make a little money of my own. I hate not having my own money. I hate not feeling like I can splurge and just buy something for me. I hate charging your birthday present on our credit card and then paying the bill out of *your* paycheck."

"Kate, it's not my money or your money. It's our money. You know that."

"Well, maybe so. But when I get my part-time job, it's going to be *my* money."

"Why don't you run an ad and try to find a sitter one day a week? Or swap with Kari, start the babysitting co-op you've been talking about."

"Dave, it's not that easy. We have three kids aged four and under. Who's going to want to swap?"

"Why don't you go back to work? It sounds like that's what you're really saying. And if that's what you want and you're ready to do that, I'm all for it. You know that."

But that wasn't really what I wanted either. I wanted to make being at home work for me...work for us.

We went around and around in circles until finally we started to work things out.

Setting new rules at home

I realized the answer was not for Dave to give up his outside interests and activities. He needed them as much as I did. And when push came to shove, I didn't want him resenting me because all he did was work and come home to take care of the kids. And he came to terms with not playing golf *every* Saturday morning. We now switch off Saturday mornings.

And I'm letting go of some of the "chore" stuff I had taken on — laundry, making the beds, etc. I don't feel compelled any more to do the chores around the house simply because I've chosen a career at home with our kids. Dave now cooks dinner two nights a week, I cook two nights a week, and we wing it the other nights. It really helps. He shares in laundry. He gives the kids a bath every night and puts them to bed while I work on this book, get organized for the next day, or relax with the ritual of my nightly bubble bath. "Calgon take(s) me away..."

In addition, I've had to find out how to get some time for myself to pursue my interests or run some errands alone. I started swapping kids for one afternoon or one morning a week with my neighbor, which wasn't as hard as I had thought. Now we both have our own time to run errands, plan a meeting for our volunteer work, or meet a friend for coffee. I also know that many of my friends have started neighborhood co-ops by putting up ads at dry-cleaners, churches, and sticking flyers in mailboxes.

I've also found a program, Parents Morning Out, at a local church where for $2/hour you can have quality, church day-care one day a week. Those four hours each week were enough to empower me to start my publishing endeavor at home so I didn't feel like my professional aspirations had been forgotten just because I'm making my main career at home with kids. Volunteering is rewarding, but writing and publishing gives me an outlet at home that helps bring so much balance to my life. It's something I do that's tangible and just for me.

Dave and I have made a point of going over our calendars once a week and seeing what nights I have coming up for meetings, book clubs, and outings, and what nights Dave needs to get things done around the house or work late. We try to plan 3 to 4 family nights a week where we go to parks, have a silly supper, play games, or watch a movie all together.

Also, Dave and I truly discovered we needed to make an effort to get out at least every other week together, by ourselves, to talk. Between kids and outside obligations it seemed we never completed a conversation. I never believed it when I read a statistic that the average married couple talks five minutes a week. It scared me to see that becoming a reality.

We try to get a babysitter every other Wednesday and go out for a least an hour to talk. Sometimes it's a big date and dinner, others it may be just coffee. We take turns arranging the "dates" so I don't feel it's all my responsibility.

Once Dave and I started talking about how out of balance our marriage had gotten and finding solutions like splitting the chores and planning time out, I started to feel less "wife-like" and, in turn, less resentful.

FINDING BALANCE INSIDE SO I CAN FOCUS OUTSIDE

It's hard to feel like a wife. I never wanted to be one in the old-fashioned sense. I wanted to be an equal spouse. And even though I have a husband who does more around the house and with our kids than 99.9% of the dads and husbands out there, it's hard to feel equality when I'm the one home fighting the battles day in and day out with the kids.

Dave walks in the door at 6:00 pm most evenings, and no matter what the mood prior to that door opening, the kids grow big smiles and run to give him hugs shouting enthusiastically, "DADDEEE!"

Sometimes I wish it were me. I wish I could go back to being a "treat" to the kids. I wish my time with them could be special instead of ordinary. I'm here all day every day, and they tune me out faster and get sick of me more easily than they do their dad. But in the long run I'm hopeful that my ordinary presence, day in/day out, will help build a lasting closeness with the kids that makes them feel happy, secure, and loved.

As I've unraveled this "wife" role and recreated myself into a career at-home mom, I've realized I need to continue to ensure I'm getting my needs met so I don't resent being the ordinary one and resent Dave for his career and his time away. Resentment and bitterness are unhealthy for me. They make me turn inward and become self-absorbed. That was part of my problem in the airport that day over a year ago. I found I was losing my focus outward on the kids and on Dave.

I'm finding out that when my needs are met, I'm a happier, more content mother and spouse. And that bodes well for creating a happy family. And in the sum total of things, that's why

I made the decision in the first place to be a full-time mom, to work full time at making ours a happy, loving family.

AFTERWARD

It's been nine months since I wrote the first eight chapters of this book. As I've re-read and revised each of the chapters, I can see how much more I've adjusted to at-home motherhood over the past nine months. It takes time, and each day has gotten easier and more rewarding.

I've found that as I've started to fill each of the voids left in my life after leaving my career, I've grown more comfortable with myself and my career at home. I'm now proud of my job title of mother; I've found more challenges and creative outlets than I had set out to find; I've made many new friends; and Dave and I have re-created the balance in our marriage.

That doesn't mean that everything is perfect.

Now I'm facing new and different challenges. I'm teetering off to the other side of the tightrope because I've overcompensated by saying "yes" to every volunteer opportunity and every invite for the kids. All while I've attempted to try to write and publish this book. Some days I've felt like I'm taking on too much.

So like anything, full-time motherhood is a constant balancing act. I'm continually trying to figure out how much I can do for me and my work, while I still accomplish all I want to do with our kids.

I sometimes find myself reconciling the difference between what I thought my life would be and the reality of what it has become. I've given up the SuperMom image and my desire for accomplishments in the fast track corporate world, but I've also recognized that doesn't mean I have to give up my own goals.

As I've redefined myself, I'm beginning to understand that I *can* do it all, but not according to the rules that men and corporations have written. I can do it my own way, with my own rules on how parenthood in the '90s can be.

And I believe that's the only way it's going to change. As Gloria Steinem says, ours will be "a revolution from within." It starts with me first. Defining and redefining who I am as an at-home parent, just like every other parent who wants to dedicate himself/herself to their kids without losing themselves and their career ambitions.

And I'm taking my husband right along with me. As he sees me at home with the kids, it's made him think more about how he can have time at home parenting our children. We're trying to figure out a way where he can work in his own business and work from home two days a week so I can pursue my interests. I think that will elevate our quality of parenting by giving us a true partnership in raising our family.

And little by little, as families create their own ways of making it work and finding balance, we'll revolutionize the corporate world, forcing them to redefine themselves right along with us.

Because our kids are worth it. Our families our worth it.

It's fulfilling to see how much we've all grown in the past nine months since I started this book. Life at home is so different from the working world where you can see your progress as you go. Part of my struggle has been that kids don't grow and learn in daily increments, with daily results. It's only when I look back a month or two at a time that I realize how much we've learned, and all the memories we've created.

It goes too fast, and despite the ups and downs of life with children, I'm learning to cherish every moment. Tomorrow will be here soon enough, and before we know it, Dave and I will have an empty house echoing with memories. My hope is that they'll be good ones for all of us.

And I also hope that years from now, when Dave and I stand in our empty house listening to the memories, we'll be happy that we made them together. And neither one of us will feel like we gave up too much or missed out on too much. Or lost ourselves or each other along the way. That we succeeded in finding that delicate balance between briefcase and diaper bag, between work and home, between doing for family and doing for self.

I started this book thinking I had traveled to the end of the road, that my transition from briefcase to diaper bag was over. But as I close and look ahead, I realize my journey to find balance at home is really just beginning. I've come farther than I thought possible in three years, but I've still got a long road ahead of me. Who knows where I'll end up?

Katie Kelley Dorn at home, as drawn by her daughter Kelley.

Katie Kelley Dorn is an at-home mother who enjoys raising her three, soon to be four, children with her husband, Dave, in Minnetonka, Minnesota.